ANIMALS UNDERGROUND
MOLES

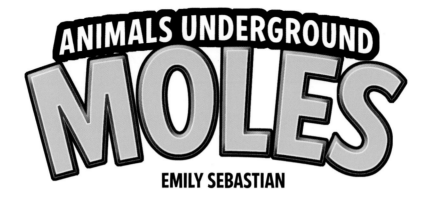

EMILY SEBASTIAN

PowerKiDS press

New York

Published in 2012 by The Rosen Publishing Group, Inc.
29 East 21st Street, New York, NY 10010

First Edition

Editor: Amelie von Zumbusch
Book Design: Julio Gil

Photo Credits: Cover, back cover (mole) Geoff du Feu/Stone/Getty Images; back cover (armadillo, fox, mongoose), pp. 4–5, 10–11, 18–19, 24 (top right) Shutterstock.com; back cover (badger) Norbert Rosing/National Geographic/Getty Images; back cover (chipmunk) James Hager/Robert Harding World Imagery/Getty Images; p. 7 © Michael Habicht/Animals Animals-Earth Scenes; p. 9 Michael Wheatley/ All Canada Photos/Getty Images; pp. 12–13, 23 iStockphoto/Thinkstock; pp. 12 (inset), 24 (bottom right) Richard Davies/Dorling Kindersley/Getty Images; pp. 15, 24 (top left) Paulo De Oliveira/Photolibrary/ Getty Images; pp. 16–17, 24 (bottom left) Hemera/Thinkstock; p. 21 Robin Redfern/Photolibrary/ Getty Images.

Library of Congress Cataloging-in-Publication Data

Sebastian, Emily.
  Moles / by Emily Sebastian. — 1st ed.
      p. cm. — (Animals underground)
  Includes index.
  ISBN 978-1-4488-4952-9 (library binding) — ISBN 978-1-4488-5054-9 (pbk.) —
ISBN 978-1-4488-5055-6 (6-pack)
  1. Moles (Animals)—Juvenile literature. I. Title.
  QL737.S76S43 2012
  599.33'5—dc22
                                        2010050091

Manufactured in the United States of America

CPSIA Compliance Information: Batch #WS11PK: For Further Information contact Rosen Publishing, New York, New York at 1-800-237-9932

CONTENTS

This is a mole. Moles live in North America, Europe, and Asia.

Star-nosed moles live in eastern North America. They learn about things by touching them with their noses.

Coast moles live in western North America. They are most active in the winter.

Cats are the pets that most often hunt moles. Wild animals, such as **hawks**, also hunt moles.

Moles spend most of their time underground. They dig long **tunnels**.

Moles dig very fast. They dig with their **claws**.

Moles can make a mess of your yard! They dig up piles of dirt, called **molehills**.

Moles like dirt that is a little wet. It is easy to dig through.

Moles do not see well. They find food by its smell.

Worms are a mole's main food.
Moles eat bugs, too.

23

Words to Know

claws

hawk

molehills

tunnels

Index

Web Sites

Due to the changing nature of Internet links, PowerKids Press has developed an online list of Web sites related to the subject of this book. This site is updated regularly. Please use this link to access the list:
www.powerkidslinks.com/anun/moles/